My Canada
NUNAVUT

By Sheila Yazdani

TABLE OF CONTENTS

Nunavut 3

Glossary 22

Index 24

A Crabtree Seedlings Book

Crabtree Publishing
crabtreebooks.com

School-to-Home Support for Caregivers and Teachers

This book helps children grow by letting them practice reading. Here are a few guiding questions to help the reader build his or her comprehension skills. Possible answers appear in red.

Before Reading:

- What do I know about Nunavut?
  - *I know that Nunavut is a territory.*
  - *I know that Nunavut can be very cold.*

- What do I want to learn about Nunavut?
  - *I want to learn what activities I can do in Nunavut.*
  - *I want to learn what the official flag looks like.*

During Reading:

- What have I learned so far?
  - *I have learned that Iqaluit is the capital of Nunavut.*
  - *I have learned that the Penny Ice Cap is at Auyuittuq National Park.*

- I wonder why…
  - *I wonder why the official flower is the purple saxifrage.*
  - *I wonder why there is an inuksuk on Nunavut's flag.*

After Reading:

- What did I learn about Nunavut?
  - *I have learned that you can go dogsledding in Naujaat.*
  - *I have learned that the official animal is the Canadian Inuit dog.*

- Read the book again and look for the glossary words.
  - *I see the word **capital** on page 6, and the word **explorer** on page 18. The other glossary words are found on pages 22 and 23.*

I live in Iqaluit. I can see the northern lights in the sky in the winter.

The signs in my city are in English, French, and **Inuktitut**.

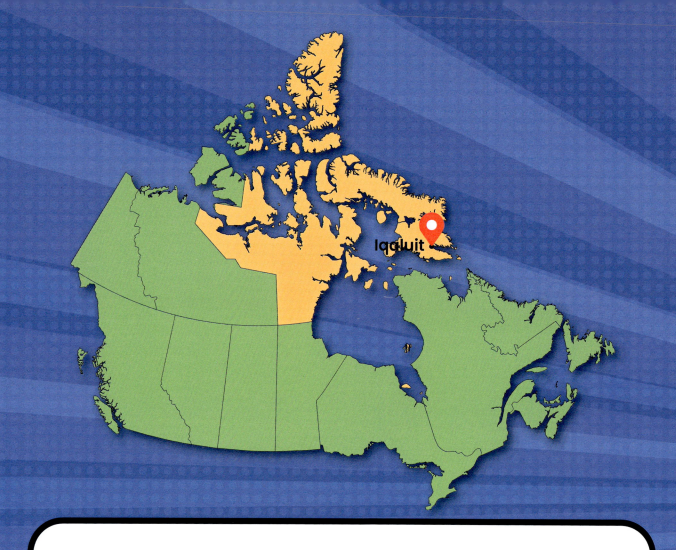

Nunavut is a **territory** in northern Canada. The **capital** is Iqaluit.

Fun Fact: Iqaluit is the largest city in Nunavut, but the smallest capital in Canada.

The official animal is the Canadian Inuit dog.

Fun Fact: Arctic char is the most popular fish to catch and eat in Nunavut.

My territory's flag is yellow and white. A red **inuksuk** is in the middle.

Nunavut has the longest **coastline** in Canada!

My family enjoys hiking at Auyuittuq National Park. I like to see the Penny Ice Cap.

Fun Fact: Auyuittuq means "the land that never melts" in Inuktitut.

Visiting Quttinirpaaq National Park with my family is exciting! Sometimes we see Arctic hares.

I like learning about history while walking on the Northwest Passage Trail. I pretend I am an **explorer**.

Fun Fact: For hundreds of years, explorers tried to find a passage that connected the Atlantic Ocean to the Pacific Ocean through the Arctic Ocean. This became known as the Northwest Passage.

I like to go dogsledding in Naujaat.

Glossary

capital (CAP-ih-tuhl): The city or town where the government of a country, state, or province is located

coastline (KOAST-lien): The area where land meets the ocean

explorer (ek-SPLOR-ur): A person who travels to a place no one has been before to learn more about it